J

COUNTRY PROFILES

THE

CZECH REPUBLIC

BY ALICIA Z. KLEPEIS

BELLWETHER MEDIA • MINNEAPOLIS, MN

Blastoff! Discovery launches a new mission: reading to learn. Filled with facts and features, each book offers you an exciting new world to explore!

BLASTOFF! UNIVERSE

BLASTOFF! DISCOVERY

BLASTOFF! Beginners

BLASTOFF! READERS

GRADE K

GRADES 1-3

GRADE 4

This edition first published in 2021 by Bellwether Media, Inc.

No part of this publication may be reproduced in whole or in part without written permission of the publisher.
For information regarding permission, write to Bellwether Media, Inc., Attention: Permissions Department,
6012 Blue Circle Drive, Minnetonka, MN 55343.

Library of Congress Cataloging-in-Publication Data

Names: Klepeis, Alicia, 1971- author.
Title: The Czech Republic / by Alicia Z. Klepeis.
Description: Minneapolis, MN : Bellwether Media, Inc., 2021. |
    Series: Blastoff! Discovery: Country Profiles | Includes
    bibliographical references and index. | Audience: Ages 7-13 |
    Audience: Grades 4-6 | Summary: "Engaging images accompany
    information about the Czech Republic. The combination of high-
    interest subject matter and narrative text is intended for students in
    grades 3 through 8." Provided by publisher.
Identifiers: LCCN 2020001628 (print) | LCCN 2020001629
    (ebook) | ISBN 9781644872529 (library binding) | ISBN
    9781681037158 (ebook)
Subjects: LCSH: Czech Republic–Juvenile literature.
Classification: LCC DB2011 .K55 2021 (print) | LCC DB2011
    (ebook) | DDC 943.71–dc23
LC record available at https://lccn.loc.gov/2020001628
LC ebook record available at https://lccn.loc.gov/2020001629

Editor: Kieran Downs   Designer: Brittany McIntosh

Printed in the United States of America, North Mankato, MN.

TABLE OF CONTENTS

PICTURESQUE PRAGUE

PRAGUE CASTLE
PRAGUE

It is a cool morning as a group of **tourists** arrives in Prague. They start the day at Prague Castle, which stands above the Vltava River. This huge complex was built more than one thousand years ago. The group admires the **architecture** of the Old Royal Palace.

OTHER TOP SITES

BOHEMIAN SWITZERLAND NATIONAL PARK

KLEMENTINUM LIBRARY

ŘÍP MOUNTAIN

TELČ HISTORIC CENTER

In the afternoon, the group walks down to St. Nicholas Church. Its huge copper dome can be seen from a distance. Later, they picnic at Kampa, an island park on the river. As the sun sets, they stand on the Charles Bridge to take photos. Welcome to the Czech Republic!

LOCATION

The Czech Republic is located in central Europe. It covers 30,451 square miles (78,867 square kilometers). Prague, the Czech capital, is near the country's center. The booming city of Brno lies in the southeast.

The Czech Republic is **landlocked**. Germany borders the Czech Republic to the west and the north. Poland is also a neighbor to the north. The country of Slovakia lies southeast of the Czech Republic. Austria makes up the southern border.

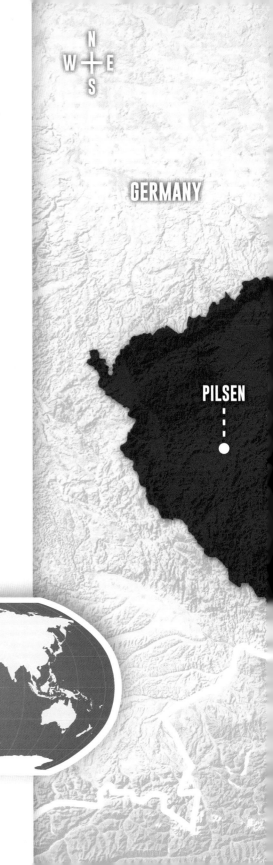

GERMANY

PILSEN

POLAND

★ - - - PRAGUE

OSTRAVA - - - ●

THE
CZECH REPUBLIC

● - - - BRNO

SLOVAKIA

AUSTRIA

LANDSCAPE AND CLIMATE

Most of the Czech Republic is made up of the Bohemian **Plateau**. Low mountain ranges surround this huge area. The Sudeten Mountains run east to west along the Polish border. The vast Bohemian Forest is in the country's southwest.

The Czech Republic has many rivers. The Elbe flows northwest into Germany. The Vltava River is the country's longest.

VLTAVA RIVER

ELBE RIVER

N W E S

= BOHEMIAN PLATEAU   = SUDETEN MOUNTAINS

SUDETEN MOUNTAINS

TOO HOT TO HANDLE

In 2019, a new record was set for the highest June temperature ever recorded in the Czech Republic. It reached 102 degrees Fahrenheit (38 degrees Celsius) in the village of Doksany, which is northwest of Prague.

VLTAVA RIVER

PRAGUE

Average seasonal highs and lows

JANUARY
HIGH: 36 °F (2 °C)
LOW: 25 °F (-4 °C)

APRIL
HIGH: 57 °F (14 °C)
LOW: 39 °F (4 °C)

JULY
HIGH: 73 °F (23 °C)
LOW: 55 °F (13 °C)

OCTOBER
HIGH: 55 °F (13 °C)
LOW: 41 °F (5 °C)

°F = degrees Fahrenheit
°C = degrees Celsius

The Czech Republic has a **continental** climate. Its summers can be hot and **humid**. The hottest months also receive the most rainfall. Winters are cold. Ice and freezing rain are common. Snow often falls in the mountains.

WILDLIFE

The Czech Republic is home to a wide variety of wildlife. In the forests and fields, red deer munch on ferns and berries as geese soar overhead. Pine martens search for birds, squirrels, and berries to eat. Otters, hares, and wild boars are other common animals in the Czech Republic.

The Czech Republic's border with Slovakia is a wildlife-rich area. Beavers use trees to build their lodges. Spined loach swim in the Thaya and Morava Rivers. Beetles crawl among the oaks while fire-bellied toads seek out insects on the surface of waters nearby.

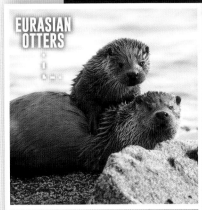

EURASIAN OTTERS

FIRE-BELLIED TOAD

WILD BOAR

PROTECTING THE LYNX

The lynx is a rare but beautiful big cat. In the 1940s and 1950s, they were nearly wiped out in the Czech Republic. Efforts to protect the lynx have been successful. Today, about 50 to 70 lynx roam the Czech Republic's mountains.

PINE MARTEN

Life Span: up to 10 years
Red List Status: least concern

pine marten range =

LEAST CONCERN	NEAR THREATENED	VULNERABLE	ENDANGERED	CRITICALLY ENDANGERED	EXTINCT IN THE WILD	EXTINCT

More than 10 million people live in the Czech Republic. Almost two out of three Czechs belong to the Czech **ethnic** group. A smaller number of Moravian and Slovak people live there, too. More than one in four people in the Czech Republic do not identify with one specific group.

12

The Czech Republic has no official religion. Only about one out of ten Czechs are Christian. More than one out of three Czechs are **atheist**. Czech is the country's official language. But Czech students also start learning English in elementary school.

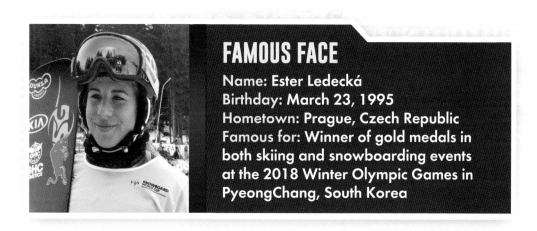

FAMOUS FACE

Name: Ester Ledecká
Birthday: March 23, 1995
Hometown: Prague, Czech Republic
Famous for: Winner of gold medals in both skiing and snowboarding events at the 2018 Winter Olympic Games in PyeongChang, South Korea

SPEAK CZECH

ENGLISH	CZECH	HOW TO SAY IT
hello	dobrý den	DO-bree den
goodbye	na shledanou	NAH skleh-dah-noh
please	prosím	PROH-seem
thank you	děkuji	DYEH-koo-yih
yes	ano	AH-no
no	ne	neh

BRNO

About three out of four Czechs live in **urban** areas. Prague is the country's largest city, with over one million people. Most people in Czech cities live in apartment buildings. They often travel by bus, train, or **tram**. More and more people are buying their own cars. Houses in the countryside are often made of brick. They typically have gardens, too.

CHILDREN'S ISLAND

Within the city of Prague are several islands on the Vltava River. Children's Island, or *Detský ostrov*, has a lot of playground equipment. It also has tennis and basketball courts.

TRAM
PRAGUE

People in the Czech Republic often have fewer children than in most countries. Families tend to be smaller in urban areas than in the countryside. Grandparents often live with their children and grandchildren.

People in the Czech Republic dress like those in other parts of
Europe or the United States. At festivals, however, Czechs may
wear **traditional** costumes. These outfits vary by region. Folk
costumes in Blata have very detailed **embroidery**. Costumes
in Doudlebsko feature yellow trousers made of deerskin, blue
knitted stockings, and buckled shoes.

The polka is a popular dance and type of music in the Czech Republic. It started in the mid-1800s in the Bohemia region. Accordions, trumpets, and a tuba typically play in polka bands. Even today, Czech festivals often have polka dancing and music!

FORTUNE-TELLING APPLES

At Christmastime, some Czechs use apples to tell the future. They cut an apple in half and look at the core. A star-shaped core signals a bright future.

POLKA BAND

PRAGUE FUNFAIR ORCHESTRA

Young children in the Czech Republic may attend preschool. Elementary school starts at age 6. Students are required to go to school from first through ninth grade. Most Czech students go on to high schools. This prepares students for college or work.

About 6 out of 10 Czechs have **service jobs**. Many of these jobs are in the tourism industry. Others are in banks, offices, or hospitals. Farmers grow grains, sugar beets, potatoes, and fruit. They also make dairy products such as butter and cheese. Other workers **manufacture** products including cars, chemicals, and machinery.

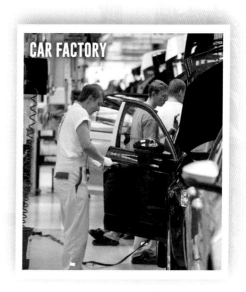

CAR FACTORY

GORGEOUS GLASSWARE

The Czech Republic is famous for its beautiful glassware. Factories produce everything from drinking glasses to jewelry. Glass Christmas ornaments are also made.

SOCCER

Soccer is the most popular sport in the Czech Republic. Some cities have their own professional teams. Small villages have their own local teams. Czechs also enjoy ice hockey, tennis, and swimming. Hiking and camping are popular activities for nature-loving Czechs. In the wintertime, people enjoy both downhill and cross-country skiing. The town of Lipno has one of the world's longest ice-skating tracks. It is more than 6 miles (10 kilometers) long!

HIKING

Czech children enjoy playing on their computers and phones. Watching television is popular, too. Czech people like spending time with friends at cafés and restaurants. Close friends and family members may be invited to dinner at home.

CAFÉ

MAKE A DOUGH ORNAMENT

Dough ornaments have often decorated Czech homes during the holiday season. Have an adult help you with the baking part of this craft.

What You Need:

- 2 cups flour
- 1/2 cup water
- 1/2 cup vinegar
- 1 egg yolk
- parchment paper
- a cookie sheet
- a straw
- a small paintbrush
- string or ribbon
- a bowl
- a spoon

Instructions:

1. Put the flour, water, and vinegar into a bowl and mix well with a spoon to make the dough.
2. Add one tablespoon of water and knead the dough until flexible. Let it rest for an hour.
3. Take small chunks of dough and make ornaments of whatever shapes you wish. Use the straw to make holes near the top.
4. Let the ornaments dry completely on the cookie sheet.
5. When dry, brush each ornament with a mixture made from one egg yolk and one tablespoon of water.
6. Bake on a parchment paper-lined cookie sheet at 280 degrees Fahrenheit (138 degrees Celsius) for about 20 minutes. The ornaments should be a golden color.
7. Hang each ornament from a string or ribbon. Enjoy!

21

A UNIQUE SODA

Kofola is one of the best-selling beverages in the Czech Republic. This cola-type soda is very sweet and tastes like licorice. It also comes in other flavors, such as vanilla and lemon.

Traditional Czech food takes a lot of work to prepare. A common dish is roast beef served in cream sauce with dumplings. Sauerkraut, made with chopped cabbage pickled in salty water, is featured in many Czech meals.

People in the Czech Republic eat a variety of stews and soups. *Bramborová polévka* is a soup containing potato, chicken stock, mushrooms, and herbs. *Goulash* is a hearty stew containing pork or beef, paprika, and dumplings. Popular desserts include apple strudel and honey cake. People also enjoy fruit-filled dumplings.

SAUERKRAUT

GOULASH

MORAVIAN MOLASSES COOKIES

Moravia is a region in the eastern Czech Republic. It is known for these sweet, spicy cookies. Have an adult help you make this recipe.

Ingredients:
1/3 cup molasses
2 tablespoons brown sugar
3 tablespoons vegetable shortening
1/2 teaspoon ground ginger
1/2 teaspoon cinnamon
1/2 teaspoon salt
1/2 teaspoon baking soda
1 1/4 cups flour

Steps:
1. Combine all ingredients except the flour in a large bowl until well blended.

2. Slowly add in the flour until it is all mixed in. The dough will be stiff.

3. Cover the bowl and place in the fridge to chill for about 4 hours.

4. Preheat the oven to 375 degrees Fahrenheit (191 degrees Celsius). Roll the dough into four balls.

5. Flatten one ball at a time to about 1/8-inch thick.

6. Use a cookie cutter or the rim of a cup to cut the dough into circles. Place these onto a greased cookie sheet.

7. Bake for about 6 minutes until the cookies are slightly brown. Enjoy!

CELEBRATIONS

People in the Czech Republic start the year by celebrating New Year's Day. They have big parties with family and friends. People exchange **marzipan** candies. They also give each other pig-shaped paper cards for good luck in the coming year. Fireworks are another part of New Year's fun.

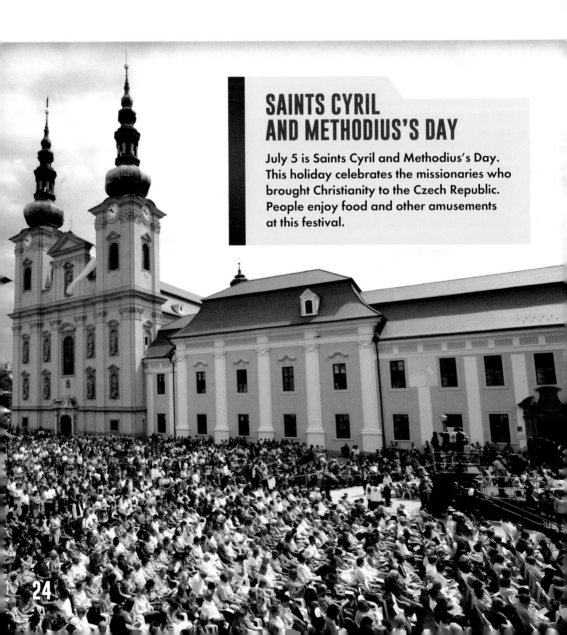

SAINTS CYRIL AND METHODIUS'S DAY

July 5 is Saints Cyril and Methodius's Day. This holiday celebrates the missionaries who brought Christianity to the Czech Republic. People enjoy food and other amusements at this festival.

EASTER
EGGS

As part of their Easter celebrations, Czechs decorate eggs. People use dye to paint flowers and other shapes. Special Easter foods include a sweet bread called *mazanec*. Christmas markets are a festive part of the holiday season. People buy decorations, Christmas trees, and traditional foods like carp. Czechs celebrate their **culture** and country throughout the year!

TIMELINE

1526
The Habsburg Dynasty begins their almost 400-year rule over Bohemia

500s CE
The Slavs arrive in present-day Moravia and Slovakia

AROUND 500 BCE
The Celts arrive and settle in what is now the Czech Republic

1939
Germany begins a 6-year occupation of Czechoslovakia

1918
The new country of Czechoslovakia is proclaimed

1346
King Charles IV is crowned king, starting the peak of the kingdom of Bohemia

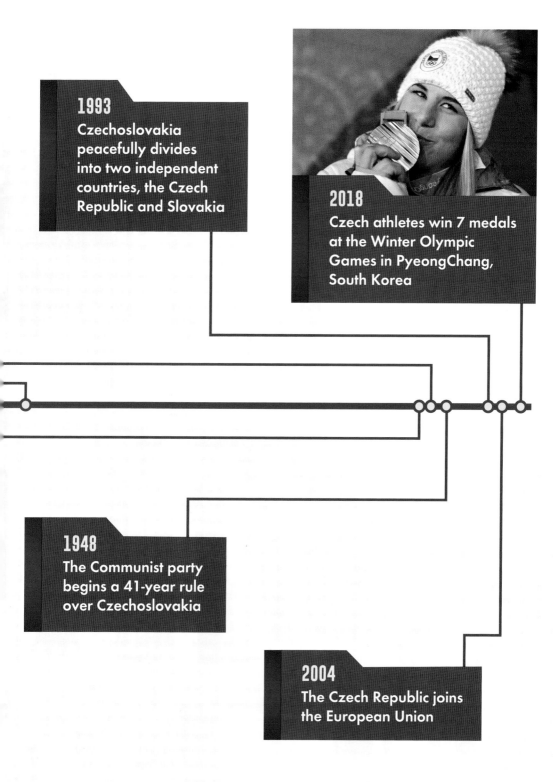

1993
Czechoslovakia peacefully divides into two independent countries, the Czech Republic and Slovakia

2018
Czech athletes win 7 medals at the Winter Olympic Games in PyeongChang, South Korea

1948
The Communist party begins a 41-year rule over Czechoslovakia

2004
The Czech Republic joins the European Union

Official Name: The Czech Republic

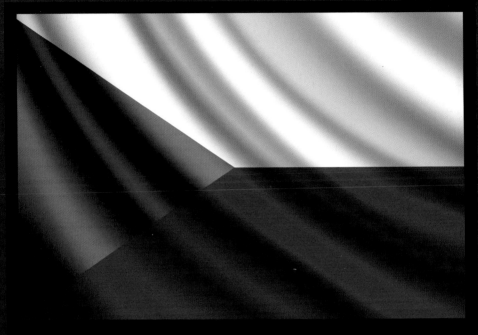

Flag of the Czech Republic: The Czech Republic's flag has two equal-sized horizontal stripes. The top stripe is white. The bottom stripe is red. A blue triangle is found on the left side of the flag. Red and white are Bohemia's traditional colors. Blue is Slovakia's traditional color. The blue and white also represent the roles of France and the United States in helping the country gain independence.

Area: 30,451 square miles
(78,867 square kilometers)

Capital City: Prague

Important Cities: Brno, Ostrava, Pilsen

Population:
10,702,498 (July 2020)

WHERE PEOPLE LIVE

COUNTRYSIDE
25.9%

CITY
74.1%

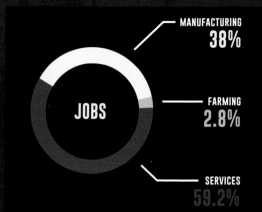

MANUFACTURING
38%

JOBS

FARMING
2.8%

SERVICES
59.2%

Main Exports:

chemicals

cars

computers

animal food

vehicle parts

National Holiday:
Czechoslovak Independence Day
(October 28)

Main Language:
Czech

Form of Government:
parliamentary republic

Title for Country Leaders:
president (head of state)
prime minister (head of government)

RELIGION

OTHER
54%

ROMAN
CATHOLIC
10.4%

PROTESTANT
1.1%

NONE
34.5%

Unit of Money:
Czech koruna

GLOSSARY

architecture—the style in which buildings are designed and built

atheist—related to a belief that God does not exist

continental—related to a relatively dry climate with very cold winters and very hot summers

culture—the beliefs, arts, and ways of life in a place or society

embroidery—the art of decorating things with patterns sewn on with thread

ethnic—related to a group of people who share customs and an identity

humid—damp or moist

landlocked—enclosed or almost completely enclosed by land

manufacture—to make products, often with machines

marzipan—a sweet paste made from almonds, sugar, and egg whites

plateau—an area of flat, raised land

service jobs—jobs that perform tasks for people or businesses

tourists—people who travel to visit another place

traditional—related to customs, ideas, or beliefs handed down from one generation to the next

tram—a passenger vehicle powered by electricity from an overhead cable

urban—related to cities and city life

TO LEARN MORE

AT THE LIBRARY

Rechner, Amy. *Germany*. Minneapolis, Minn.: Bellwether Media, 2018.

Seavey, Lura Rogers. *Czech Republic*. New York, N.Y.: Children's Press, 2018.

Sioras, Efstathia. *Czech Republic*. New York, N.Y.: Cavendish Square, 2018.

ON THE WEB

FACTSURFER

Factsurfer.com gives you a safe, fun way to find more information.

1. Go to www.factsurfer.com.

2. Enter "Czech Republic" into the search box and click Q.

3. Select your book cover to see a list of related content.

INDEX